700
F

HOUSEHOLD MECHANICS

New Issues Poetry & Prose

Editor	Herbert Scott
Associate Editor	David Dodd Lee
Advisory Editors	Nancy Eimers, Mark Halliday, William Olsen, J. Allyn Rosser
Assistants to the Editor	Rebecca Beech, Derek Pollard, Jonathan Pugh, Marianne E. Swierenga
Assistant Editors	Erik Lesniewski, Lydia Melvin, Adela Najarro, Margaret von Steinen
Editorial Assistants	Jennifer Abbott, Bethany Salgat
Business Manager	Michele McLaughlin
Fiscal Officer	Marilyn Rowe

New Issues Poetry & Prose
The College of Arts and Sciences
Western Michigan University
Kalamazoo, MI 49008

First Edition, 2002.

ISBN	1-930974-16-7 (paperbound)

Library of Congress Cataloging-in-Publication Data:
Mangold, Sarah
Household Mechanics/Sarah Mangold
Library of Congress Control Number: 2001132696

Art Direction	Joseph Wingard
Design	Casey McLellan
Production	Paul Sizer
	The Design Center, Department of Art
	College of Fine Arts
	Western Michigan University
Printing	Courier Corporation

HOUSEHOLD MECHANICS

SARAH MANGOLD

FOREWORD BY C.D. WRIGHT

New Issues

WESTERN MICHIGAN UNIVERSITY

Foreword

Awareness begins at home, "eye level with the cake," or so one could infer from Sarah Mangold's *Household Mechanics*, a disquieting review of indirect disclosures, internal churnings, and palpable notions, subjected to a tense and skeletal language. She probes, evokes but chooses not to describe or elaborate. She "pulls across," which she distinguishes from "associating with." The voice is consistent, distant. The sentence is disjointed; the thinking continuous.

None of us knows where poetry is going. Everyone who is undertaking to write it now is making their large or small machine out of ordered and scavenged parts. Reading *Household Mechanics* affords the experience of getting in, sometimes falling in, of going forward, going somewhere. To go is key. To go is essential. The suitcases are permanently packed. "Reading homes explode." The difficulties are not difficult to construe—in reading homes.

The subjective ground is respected and dissected, alternately and simultaneously. I could not tell you what is in that cake, but it keeps appearing. Of course it could be strategized another way: this is hers, her way "to get the boys to pass you the ball" among countless alternatives. Possibility holds a special place in Sarah Mangold's book—for possibility can be seized upon by the "keenness of the third eye" or can be pluralized. Possibilities can create openings such as dream holes, which are not mentioned, but I am reminded of them, architecturally. Windows are perceived, punched out where there were solid walls. And in landscape architecture, paths are worn, not where laid out, but by the walker. Dream holes, dream lines. Or perhaps in the poet Mangold's case, "it's more of a hope." The opening she sees, the openings she creates are individualized units of hope.

When I think of an obvious alignment, I think of the Objectivists. Especially, the lone woman affiliated, the geographical isolate, Niedecker. I had always wished there were more of them, because they introduced a brand of lucidity, rare, oh rare in these dis-united states of poetry. This is "not an airshow." This is household mechanics. This living; it takes a lifetime.

—C.D. Wright

Contents

Acknowledgments

Thanks to the editors of the following publications where these poems first appeared:

Aufgabe: "Destinations"

can we have our ball back: "Household Mechanics," "How to Approach the Volume of a Place," "Temporary Splint"

Flash+Card: "Story"

Fourteen Hills: The San Francisco State University Review: "Architecture of This City"

Outlet: "The mass of the mechanics"

Potes & Poets Press chapbook series: "Blood Substitutes"

Slope: "Ecstatic Turtlenecks," "Halfway House," "Story"

Transfer: "Baked Alaska"

Thanks also to Myung Mi Kim, Michael Palmer, and C.D. Wright.

Household Mechanics

He hid in plain sight
his own highest hopes
wearing the red scarf

They had rehearsed it
blue ski parka
clutch of photographs
the formative event of his childhood
taken to the railroad station

He maintained a journal
his real name
safely stashed in Scarsdale
Most of the spoken words
modest wooden houses
well-ordered chimneys
The details of the dancing
in the same pleasant tone
But his first alcoholic beverage
turkey with all the trimmings

Then, there's the sound
your eye right up to the screen
a slight breeze in the back of the house
the difference between spinning records

Sitting on the porch
Violet has her suitcase
in her bouncy way
feeling guilty about the string beans
and at least for now how she breathes
as someone always will
This sense of life relatively safe
the service road everyone secretly knows

And this is not about
her placement as a showgirl
and then to medical school
I can't stand those eyes
whipped up and let down
hundreds of vacant chairs
taking piano lessons

The agonizing storytelling technique
of the pencilmakers themselves
Lots of parked cars in the arms of her own home

I'd change my clothes
Assume the weight of tragedy
that a girl makes whose gown seems the awful truth
The feel of it in these terms
the need to be redeemed in the flesh
kissing each other's rings

Here was the theology

He forgot about the girl
her allegedly poor piano technique
Once a sport of kings
set in the neighborhoods she lived in
"But I do abuse you"
"I thought so"

Story: some fairy tales I'm missing
            ballast between
            peach pants
            bottled
            want to fall into his interests
            it's the salt I'm familiar with
            the brains of the operation

The mass of the mechanics

a way to use the dictionary or your interest
the world's longest floating bridge
placing your hand before the chickens
young and variable readings with newer messages
dispersion or previous experience
re-carpeting paths to doors
the only person I know and similar models

Baked Alaska

By the luck of the draw
Nora doesn't drive
miscast and so indifferent
see herself in their shoes
a small bag over her arm
her daughter's skin
other striking similarities
still awaiting tissue confirmation

She has a big smile
her bread and butter
the curtains, the corners
off her tongue

What is most significant
our man is in a fix
this man is not obsessed
sausages and eggs and bacon

We expect to see something happen
by marrying the wrong man
stripped to its essentials
the staircase at the back of the stage

We might imagine
the yarns he spins about her
a posse of armed horsemen
a portentous whisper
like a crocodile on the sand
more or less varied and delicious

The dogs all got along fine
a car missed a turn
cattle were sold
often chained together
they sat at a table
a superheated soul

her feelings in print take hostages
their fortunes rose and fell
between the rooms people live in

Make the trip
make a great impression
just get up and be witty

she will often float
in genuine Atlantic sea water

See how people actually live
Hawaii and its controversies
head in a box of salt
paper in the oven

In this period
have the nerve to suggest
a modest house
carving knives

you got to learn to breathe

Story

I.

since he was a baby
a small amount of money
its strange lips
appears on the porch

one box to another
to put it bluntly

a beautiful idea

the interesting question
it somehow does

now they wonder what
putting on a brave face
head in the cake

to trace an account that her father
what was needed
but you never know

II.

The roots of her obsession
He seemed grateful

She smoked while she talked
The truth from me

Some of this stuff
We want to know

There will be no winners
Capable of deep love

He was right, of course
When, for example, I earnestly asked

Stay like that
Consciously changing nothing

Being a star student

Halfway House

I recognize the dangers
Italian shoes and a British suit
throwaway relationships
organized and armed
I had no idea

Then there was Ed himself
we grinned nervously at our table
exposing bathtub rings
magnificent income
huge hot pastrami sandwiches
or tomato soup

how close they are
the steps are small

Consider the damage done by purple
sound of money being burned
their prerecorded existence
hand-sewn luggage

Say the choice were made
possessing only the vaguest notion
to twirl one's fingers
but because we have grown so breathlessly
is an official language
cured or suppressed

the electricity they need
brought the house down

Yearn for a period in history when
people say to themselves
We must act now
there's a nonstop demand

Driving west until the road turned
uncertain highway
we have been led to believe

I previously had been blind

Ecstatic Turtlenecks

Luckily enough recently
and across the street
the word perpetual
but I trust her
leaving the conservatory
empty brackets and access roads
singular nature of her chords
bear claws
play the whole sonata
and play it well
will get you as far as
you'd be the keyboard
and thank you
every fourth day
every third day
bit or anchor
eight pound cleat
in your shoes
when it arrived
review the marriage
out of the way
close the book
and let's say
far reaching
do you think
suspect
potatoes put in
imperfection or laceration
translations
to her work
closet onion eater
accusing him of codes
I was the worst scientist

Architecture of This City

A man comes to our house
"I know that wonder boy of yours
he won a silver spoon for his pears"
the pressure of this discovery
Here were people who had authority
They had their dogs drowned in circumstances
but I am always thinking
English it's more a percussive habit
a woman who infuriates her father
a sort of bendy battlefield
absent-minded, like a park

He seemed to speak
sadness that does not seem to be
among these people
habits of his own country
side effects such as slight rash
frescoes and indoor plumbing

Boy scouts slept beneath the stars
suspended in time and space
spaces are either segregated
even socially awkward

The scale model with all the little people
collisions for public consumption
Philip is an anthropologist
Alice is a particle physicist
how to play to or on that feeling
the writers just went to sleep
you can spin lazily
where everyone knows his place

Ever since the closet door swung ajar
There's no fixed path
all you have to do is drive

Just look

How to Approach the Volume of a Place

Pa's home was up—the devil was down

and making meals from the back of soup cans
(bound to be) utensil

(slip)
trellis

write around the rickshaw

complete transcription: knees, orange curtains
circular after
dust biting
secret of trying
could be sister again

how quiet it is when they stop

rental space
darker and dancing
(ask)
mistaken k's

they've already run over three cranes
tram

eye level with the cake. nice for awhile. my monkey friend.
back door and gazelles—wild dogs and hoofed
shallow moat
chainlink walking in

she knew his hand years before

where she is
(assuming)
swingable
not apparent it's real
no ice

wire we didn't finish
see becomes mine
waiting no one says

bruised ankles
transparent—re-enactment
my wagon as hostage

twine
gun

nothing about walking—relocation

nothing about the house
cheese entitlements

burning papers
most everyone
what that meant

Temporary Splint

enamel proteins
bone around the dog's tooth
increase in connective tissue
really excited were the dentists
optimum boneless dogs
competence factors
her pattern of exclusion
obviously implicit
the breadth of it
she circled
dare we say
pidgined

Destinations

1. Topeka

Where the problems lie.
knowing your house before you do.

stomping what goes on. and no one can go on like that.
not the treatment please. so similar. so familiar.

yes it will be fascinating.
the surgical rotation. yes they do. and as if to go through that.

so the initials. what he went through for his mother.
could see the similarities. how it accumulates.

Steve's turtle down the mud. string around his waist.
photos and all.

this is the furniture of the place. that singular apartment in town.
nothing cohesive yet. across the ditch.

2. Between the Generators

what you think of the plumper friend.
leash laws and muffler laws.
what this is. who they are.
if you want to change your major. and other keys.

she picked up on. orange and lemon in different languages.
heat. a tree house. gravel—the varieties.
tar. shoes. ditches. that kind of thing.

the field where the cows never grow.

flat house. barbed wire. spelling mistake.
no sheep. birds against the windows. something drowning in there.

3. Lake Okoboji

Me in the Marines. that was a joke in the first place.
I hate the sea. I love to sail.
I hate the water. *I understand.* and my brother had to throw me in.
off the dock and then pull me out. how it works.
heat. the small of the back. pressure. getting to know your type.
if they offer it again. I'm going to spit this stuff out.
this will require going back. something stunted like that.
something about fire.
there if there is a place to land.
every hospital visit. every parking lot there ever was.
tornado. it's that close. birds walk in. dogs across sand.

4. (   )

what passes through. these women, he's charming. charming
right now.

the prospects. cells replace—release. full circle was it.

dash. instead infatuation. how she slipped away. didn't notice the
jealousy.

what you thought. forks and spoons. all the knives when you stay.

holding your skin.

5. Where you get comfortable with it

blacking out. that's it. that'a girl.
living like. pick up artist. through my skin.
into the blood stream. an emptier car.
he's looking for the pretty girls.
line up at the bar. do you expect something from this.
a plethora of buses—running the same paths.
the same things fall out.
just us women. across the radio. who you thought you saw.
want to go down that road.
except for driving tests. where you see the turn.
they call it in the median.
because it's that social. was no meal for a drive.
and then I took him downtown.
the associations through the window.

Blood Substitutes

(10/96-12/96)

lure. elapse.   stops where

copy follow—is it a map

number three. waiting for lefty.
knock three times.   slow

   the roof on fire

how to explain. topple. to spin
write, clutter the world.   this ancient man,
ground to soap. *are you allergic to daisies*, swallow

expulsion. is it a female thing, thisorthat
where do all. trick to this story to place.

Professor Grover. now I know what they think of me.
I'm the other white meat :the roof the roof: across that and now,

interesting the work. where to write what to,
lift away skeletal. relief map. new soap.
is it going to blow. the bourbon is on fire.

~

watching Mr. Ed, a history of what.
erasing words, speech. beautiful places. what must happen and
what I've intended six lines from this. for who.
    nervous, this frog wants to be happy. this frog etc.

erosion, terrain. funny all of
how it works. to speak.

these spaces whose. are they talking to him.
Eastern Zaire . . .   food aid . . .   fractious rupture

is it the earth. entire sentences possibly missing   tripping in
the dark. become whom,
speak with who. take it apart

    what this means to you—a retreat—I suspect the streets—

aside, my father. language
    coming apart,
it's deconstructing our ability. to do my own show.

the combination turned over. all about the eyes the melons and
will not meet who you were not intended

I pick the folder he didn't expect the disappointment volume.
when you are not that tall yourself, feet in the ruts

whom he loves all parties aside—to be prolific
the erasure wants to stay with her

~

books to steal. the world and labs just throw and the cast and
mold. how it will take. what is expected

    some homes explode

the weather is the same. Pakistan has way. that way to come back,
    if you wanted. to breathe.
from room. dirt circle drive. ruts from trucks

trailers. the parents document what comes.
feeding the words :poems to each other: flinging this left andright

Bosnia. unexploding mines. *how could it disappear.* and this,
the about to be seen, the about to be heard

    the give enough get enough—handmade coffins—delicacy
    to occupy space—to ask those questions

    ~

the children. sirens go make endings.
something that knows how,
          mines, kick boxing, re entering society,
meet the family. spoken, that pause with anyone.
what is appropriate. reading homes explode. to adjust this

     —lay story a lice—a phone with no ringer

snake charmer. the bull fight. uncle roy in a fez.

american journalists. skeletal. is there a comfort in similar bodies.
lift away the functions. the skeleton. who has an exoskeleton.

to work close enough not to go mad. to go somewhere.
you hear the tone before the translation.
omissions not to hurt the children

to write in black having always written, what is not.
plans we had. the six chapters. questions

                    ~

My father does not have glass feet—all this conscious
Prague—in an in—Long Island an island which is long

but the well dressed skeletons talk to the stripped
if it is all protection, to get to the organs, makes it work
for Allah: when the abductions, the older daughters freedom,

        will it fit—the increase—
        do the positive ions stay with you

the ins and outs. genocide the address.
battling the does not have glass feet. where it needs to go

~

it then as if then. the plates writing in Armenian. is hidden a
body. the wrap around lines to lift it up

didn't trust nouns or verbs—death and gold teeth
legs the women want,   to name,   for what,

   which fragments, ions, up the other staircase

sinks,
   this was attacked,
         the bag your own ribs to protect. think . . . everything
coining back. where it comes from

                              ~

well oiled, the teeth, the orthodontics of it all. to be ancient,
her spine

write out from the spine,
what English twisting it all CSI. the referral the bones.

Stein an open window

to fall right into what all   windows—all
around:between:and on:and on:the temp do the positive

hair, spines gather the bones,
     a spine to carry in the back of, consonants,
          I have vowels, hounds have vowels,   this falls

if it matters, western coffins, to know all the tricks to slavery,
have nice teeth, the partials of the, trinity who I see, still in the car
like the pictures, everything a squirrel does to a tree:
inoverthrougharound

what you chose to fall right into.
the woman with red, the price the assumption,
large enough to put spines in. processes

~

supposedly—feeling this happened—they want

eating the ink of cake the vocals becoming something . . .
spending no money being up lifting off a relative. the holy

see the squares beneath these words. to go back and forth
about a rim. cliffs depend on the dramatics

The suitcases the center of our house
the replacement walking waking to this body
you are infinitives and brown not to press are the threads

brothers some more of nope must be Cake, the best, write
sometimes the sliding chains of Sesame Street

do believe I do tell—everybody say—swallow this whole
vowels, need more vowels

of what wanting and justs waiting, yes behind,
looking for the same woman

~

is that the lake—infinitives
who you think—to spin
newink chemical—believe the speed

I sometimes :skip skip: it's about

affection it's all a fiction
I wanted—I'm—a place
wolves to the lake

definitions of where—something is happening
taking the suggestions—to sing this

~

(It's more of a hope)

the key to durability a carbon dioxide bath. problems with
abstract thinking. don't think anyone else can say that. these
moves are long. brewing with regard.

keenness of her third eye.
get the boys to pass you the ball.

There are procedures and there are procedures. must have missed
the issue. there's the scenario. I'm talking back to. don't even
know some of those words. about language. saving the day.

he's reverted.

prairie dog. prairie dog.

plural. strung out under the seat.
flamingo with the artificial leg.

~

appliances. rebates. bounce between these things.
canoeing in the Back Bay. how it turns. internal.

take her home. reduced to this. balancing. and free sandwiches.
plug it in. there you go. a bet and bacon. baby fallen off the
sofa. or balcony. *bad girl* in an accent. for effect. homogenize.

ruins and slide education. could have continued. apologizing.
harboring harbor seals. pick the century by the shoes.

~

she had her life to return to. good looking sons. subway escape
routes. wear pink. flame. wrong side of the tracks right. she
takes off. mother of the crone.

   did you disinfect your shoes. Charlie Wang. *and did it work.*
   Nadine. cold turkey. slices.
   S as in strasse.

how hard's the ball. she didn't catch. Mom says he's a mouse.
corn on the cob. serious consideration. how to control that
child. [stitching] [stitch] [suture]

take the body. collect long distance calls. those pauses aren't
someone.

play off. freight train. if the boy scouts had gone crazy.
derail. one crazed boy scout lost to the desert.
one hysterical boy scout with sand in his shoes.
low bridges. say the wrong thing. secret to it all. put against itself.
the book already read. but I got nowhere to be.

                              ~

picked over. picked on.

 well you knew me better than that. not always a happy ending.

somebody's shoe. ovens and pipes. sack of feathers. riddles on
Dixie cups. happiness has come to this. stealing her lines. not
quite satisfactory. all these places without dancing. legs. he had to
cartwheel first. somersault. *what are your questions or concerns,* took
awhile to get to this point.

something would stain. hepatitis girl. dancing with the baby.
somehow that skirt is going to make a difference.

for you a cup of cocoa. cottage cheese. up the ante. fall into. wait
up. all rather dependent. sleep it off. masquerade. along that path.
past the poles. where does that line go. tap dancing. off the guilt
train. up and running hedge rows.

~

what happens with the leftover pastry
this falling so catch
pull out the griddle
the shells pop open
smoke themselves in their own juices

cake without company. when you look back. there's another
sentence. of course it's different, and v pleats.

Tagalog. your name appears twice. flip flop.

name the child after a city. have the Great Lakes in your home.
a nervous condition.

rats run. from the sidewalk marquee. drive out here. what he'll
watch. these missing letters. your initials. engraved there. did it
explode quickly. know nothing of her life.

~

Ed's doctor told him. after his second heart attack. how did he
get that wife. from that distance. their own forensic experts.
unreliable. in the coming days.

the largest crowd ever to descend on one city. take an interest in.
where my mind could be. her friends in Ohio. greasy fingers.
failed commando raids.

now hair loss. how did they get time off. heart to God hand to
man. rescue raft. young college student. committed to.

well they're searching now certainly.

who I can subscribe to. swallow. what I'm looking for.

he's not asking why. was I the suspected thief.
precautions. prefix. suffix. throng.
what counts. what you'll wear every Monday.
trace the lineage of the word. Western concern.

~

I wouldn't recognize much up close. syncopation in the hair, dark
circles.

turning my head. where they got their trees. Western progression.
I use the term loosely. precooked after all. buried somewhere
right round.

circle. shave. toddlers in arms. small bags at the curb.
the differential equation she was looking for. I expect it to be, but
I'm taller.

rules of attraction looking for ins.

you hold your pen like it's the wrong hand. drag this hair around.
pack it up. where's the circulation. *would you like to.* the
conjunction. gather your chickens.

the early or earliest bird. terrain she enjoys. either way
dependent on maps. one direction. rare visits north.

~

use more foreign sayings so I can truly distance you. white pants
leading the way. feel the ground shake from here.

a dog among dogs
what is thrown up by his digging
best thing to do is
one thing or place or man
know more about that than is possible
barbed wire or pemmican or Paterson
exhaust—saturate—beat

I say the names, unconvincing. think we're fooling ourselves.
different set of rules.

this inscribed on my leg. his enthusiasm times 10.
she's the cheering squad. plow.

I do not have my own island off Wisconsin. does this mean I'm
responsible for another meal. what there is time for. pigs in a
blanket. Dutch flea treatment.

set up a regiment. each letter in the Italian alphabet. bird house
is imperative. serial rapist resigns from coaching girls' track
team. these are determining factors. math names. all underwear
stolen on a Sunday.

secretly waiting in the wings. an adverbial phrase. a phrase of being.

~

my life is not an airshow// burning into the screen// his
obsession with violence// talking about his wife with no ring//
she's a pretty pony// cross eyed// downy legs// so this is the
implication// walk like a building// sing my questions// I left
them flat// shave my legs// someone has to make the money//
when the dust comes up// your lips don't even stick together//
I've seen you do things backwards// there's a fire from east to
west// twinkle twinkle

. . .

tales// *that's what I like about you*// tongue through the eye
socket// so tell me again// a chicken without a happy ending//
trying to get at that sound// thump// idea on the wrists// crack
the whip// the *word* without the words// that it implies taking
your clothes off// laying down// street light// swing beat//
rescue// when you arrive// Carson City// walking down the aisle

~

logical assumptions, with every sip.

they were seriously considering. what I've made a mess of. she
must live alone. traffic comes with fog. under my eyes. driving
out his open door.

giving wrong directions. burning off the dust. making a date for.
knew what she meant. peeling of the paint.
[these people who slip in] [unravel me]

taking apart that house, down to the ornaments. those decisions
have already been made. was that her real boyfriend. did she stay
in Rome. innocuous places. repetitive stress disorder, or I'd be out
there making banners.

~

I'm right on the road. me and a pony on a boat. I could tell that
about him. some grammar rules. the event is strange.
veins and oranges.

the long term effects of that abuse. gasoline down the
throat. experiment with mittens. nothing about those brothers.

lackey. she is the star sign.
my account. Hull. husk. ripping off hairs. days with my
hands like this.

~

pulling gums. is that how you spell it. sweat between nations. *no child of mine.* she made some choices that's clear. can hope that door is. inhale. obviously not my intent.

three more hours on this stomach. she was surprised by the jealousy. ears fill up. spin off the road into low tide.

mud flaps. and it wasn't me. if we took the ferry. back and · across. drunk for ten dollars.

make me a witness, the blood is soft. extended absence. if you'd like to leave flowers. turning the card. on the bus. into three caring hands. tree pruners. *I want you quite.* I put my hand up. she doesn't have answers. he knew he'd be left.

    they both were again the idea
    900 fits and I'm running the furnace
    perpetual fever

something should be said. consistency is not my strong suit. wood shop. don't want to go to Japan. crabs and oysters. she can wait for certain things.

~

those were the legs. no candy. no costume.

why don't you become one of our readers. points off for not underlining. ruined all the chances. take you to town. gas pumps. across that bridge. cement animals. Dairy Queen. family of five with ice cream. grain elevator. water tower.

        excusing yourself to no one.

cracked timber houses. extensive rail changes. I chose this direction. populate this place. set loose. tin cars. we made her nervous.

peaches and pears. reading his mail. Egypt. that advice. cost of the call. she's growing her hair out. buoy. kite. 7-11. how they remember this part of town. forget about the path. trees. what they're expecting. noodles. not simple.

[set off alarms] [found out for the thief] [am that suspicious] [out to sea]

theory of. *sugar. sug. sugerbear.* buy guns. preserves. any eye contact. meditating on the brand of sugar. how to live that. some voices reverberate.

~

square miles. take a turn choosing the path. three kids. three
decisions. find his way back. Guthrie. just more and more trees. I
think pain killers. don't want to get the car dusty. finding fires.
they have pineapples in the bin outside. impulse buy. station
wagon under an arc of fire. over barbed wire. drove right into.

well she's dead now. her radio comes through electrical wires.
the Russian reality. blue linoleum. say insect.

your life in emergency. how do you get him ready for school.

I'd say. Ida. butterneck. sliding into knitting needles. home base.
mathematician. quarter in each pocket. slots rolling eyes. people
implode. Christmas trees. turkeys. abandoned x-rays. crashed
through the stained glass.

heart attack. some sort of name. pushed the gum down his throat.
set his days off balance. dogs of the neighborhood. legs a little
self conscious. that creek and cattle.

only because I have to go. a country and my bones aching.

~

what did she say about. that bug. mosquito. everyone fearing
sentimentality. applying for a loan. the period is for emphasis.

Every Good Boy Does Fine
All Cows Eat Grass

that's the trick. I'll explore but explaining. falls right into her.
spices as a device. eaten. a list of chores relating to and in that
language.

possible implications. announcing these expectations. writing
about funerals. *which clock is correct.* some words are the same.
inquisition. lumber jacks. driving test. leaving the house.

the time it takes to get dressed. windshield. in the shower. it's the
speed. never a seat to be found. double negative is French.
sleeping on the sofa. is it laughable.

I have seen these women. sad enough to shuffle. join in silence,
invited. bottle out of my hand.

radio system forever here. to kiss.

women in the building. waiting for thunder. shaving the humor.
black rat. does not fill him so. eating this what we get in return.

49

~

teaching in these places. *would you try to understand.* same person in new bodies. a series of best friends. what a child would enter into. start to look at. wanted her to be the adult. pour the wine.

six exercises. lukewarm rolls. salad bar. that kind of feeling. holding up the head. blindness. bulb vases. all the fish sticks you want. what does that imply for me. my burrito. fights and shoes.

for emphasis. you can start a sentence with a conjunction. the point being. and eyes like jellyfish.

give two weeks notice. pull across. different than to associate with. never answering the phone. hit rewind. lush. the single word. how do you support his actual music.

king of good intentions. because they are both beautiful. meltdown. conundrum. desperate ship. he takes all his dates here. has similar problems.

beyond this: that man transformed: heads are moving: near the walls: electrical impulse: plugging it in: I don't remember who is not to be trusted: falling for the soup: as a meal: dish up rhythm: who'll you notice: see the problem is: see what I see: back to the farm: fire: flame retardant: percolating: circulating: invited: not his voice after all: when it's wet: hock explosives: last patient of the day

(8/97-11/97)

(5/97-7/97)

belly up. domestic simplicity.
what makes it easier. he had his stories.

he took in his dry-cleaning. that girl who lived with her parents.
those powers loved her. no nothing surrounded her. made those
days.

what if I did gather my debt and leave.

she took some heat. what happened with those bees. what his
interpretations of Spain will be. glass noodles. it looked like
anything together. ask for a chair. misconception of Tibet.
meaning this city. towns that haunt. the small age not to live
there. Wichita. pressure. about your children.

who was invited they might hope. how and my train. how long
did I have to talk. 84 different delusions. take a ride in the car.
would have made a difference. *just park and leave the damage
done.* learn to say hello. this walk to meet him.

tied to the ship. the only answer real fresh potatoes.
I kept walking where it went. there may be another explanation.

they all order the seabass.
patrol. gowns. hounds.
assumed assumption. the going price.

watch the windows. confess the love.

~

a new envelope. want to go with her.
I would go to Sweden in July.

> the the the. what everything can be.
> it's all on your chair. it can all be be be.
> *Girls, listen you must divine the bees.*
> other liquids. slices of cake.

obvious eyes. smooth and smooth. blue or black attention span.
break a twenty elsewhere. as if a train. completely out of your
envelope. the notion that they will feed me soon. where I know
her from.

slip their collars. eyes and wet ears. all in a box.
suppose other locations and stops.

the books are not shelved, how could they be removed.
summer yelling. in minutes their meals and in which house.
how many are you picking. chicken bones and pig ears.

what starts happening stops happening over your salad.

it may not find you a job. jazzy cloth, but with a difference.
leatherette seats. produce important theater.
in order to do things his way. you've got to be a showman.

one must regard statements like that. clean their teeth.
now buy Gouda, pita and Dijon. fresh-frozen and flown to Tokyo.
specific rules about language.

~

Fearless fancy diving kids.
where you met your wife.

I'll read the explanation again.

raise your hand and the ride will stop. brave enough for your
sister. I will learn this in another language.

we will walk down this street.

quadruple promises. that no is a sentence.
you were in the orchard. since the German is expected.

that was only recently. what they liked.
the same hairs growing down the table.

~

bluegrass. grey hound. all the windows open.
a temperature taken. in my own kitchen stellar associates.
the story she has. who you wink wink.

hidden in walls. interspersed clapping. who was sent to buy
the limes. nothing there to drown me. certain coded personal
remarks. timecards I didn't submit. and there is her agenda.
everytime the key is turned.

filament in my pajamas. if it stands tomorrow.
the region is already under populated. that's pretty much what
happened. three or four days preparing for forays. tinfoil tiaras.
this very thing has, of course, happened. it seemed I was lost in
Sicily. knowing who is infected. silver carp and grass carp.
you know, you've seen that. and mashed potatoes like green waves.

~

confess your affections// associate with women// looks the
answer// speak of wilting and milk on lips// this should, of
course, be done quickly// if it is anyone// how would you
recognize this// to even step in that aisle// I want something
in that cup// bat and eye// how many chairs do you want//
what kind of cream cheese// decreasing your appetite// the
woman in the dress//

slight discrepancies// genes where the forks go// the reference
department cannot be replaced with an electronic brain// is
this a rescue note// I won't learn the difference// my solid
answer neatly printed

~

grow into the haircut. I could get her to marry my cousin.
pedal the gears. corners and vacant lots.

on the handlebars. spoke of. she was only being polite.
don't you think something should be done. if the messenger
never comes.

mercury in her mouth. majestic levels of investment. bandito.
using the child for betting purposes. did she learn the square
roots. Atlantic ocean. arrive in my parking lot. a good-looking
choir director never hurts. was that a burial shroud. that she
leaves the house. another part of Texas.

~

A motel room with desperate motives—dye the pages—she says she's unstoppable—the box in my arm—were you expecting this—too close to fall down fog

Lady lead house—widespread commitments—
what she does or doesn't do—
formatting questions—cemetery stayer
I'm breathing out—there's an entry for you

Small amounts of money were exchanged—she said hello

Like balloon circus animals—I'm the welcome wagon—came to certain understandings—certain minutes could be spent—my pink elephant was the agitator—comparing iced drinks—the particular music in these tables—linger—but highly likely—the animals deflate

~

Obligatory smiles—sharing chairs—a single name left out
the wood goes soft—hyphenate—whose name—whose house
for Thanksgiving

the rhythmic qualities of the ribbon—slow slight paper cuts—
run the tally—she's seven months—she doesn't speak yet—the
glass—class photo

the talker—bean grinders beyond the books
so far a tea cake—the guilt caught at a traffic light—

can they speak about her—very quickly a straw—
direct conversation—I'd put sugar on that

10 key by touch—but she is—she is
what's your baby's favorite song—just one and one
that's clear enough—in my house somewhat compressed
the orange of an orange—this might be arranged

twin hearts—buy a backyard—bullets
no later than—no older than—a dog named Quail
if I was on that corner

Well intentioned eyes—walk across this weather—
these teeth—inspired tomato sauce
where did they put the baby
firsts and seconds—lungs on the child
my time zone—three minutes
back in back in back—my dog Digger

~

fish skeletons—the side story
pick the button—buy the pants—lighten up

A detailed description of your final problem.

The experiments I didn't do etched into your skin—
pinstripes and lip liner
is she dead—and there he is
my fault arrived early—your mother arrested

they live outside the city—an oboe—
the ship is moving—what we had in common—
Bach brought the attention—the potato salad
we could transcribe each other—roots and herbs—wrinkles in
ancient magazines

only these people—slowly poisoned where
tip of the tongue—those two

Well, you're pretty enough to catch a single man.

~

places I've been—slip into the closet
he was dying here—this place—this pace—
I caught that train alone
a small envelope for summer—a direct chorus
a pension for overacting—I thought I'd be leaving

The same towns—peeled not just peaches
simple sugars—those hidden family halves
buy a cake—a plate—not her voice
evil twins of Shakespeare and then he dies
and on my hand no such luck

A cautionary tale—it's not that simple—
they have the same initials—just living here

The lip as clutch—catch the cup
what constitutes eye contact—acceptable entrances

Sarah Mangold was born in Omaha, Nebraska in 1971 and raised in Oklahoma. She received her B.A. from the University of Oklahoma and her M.F.A. from San Francisco State University. She lives in Seattle.

C.D. Wright's sixth collection of poetry, *String Light*, was selected winner of the Poetry Center Book Award. Her other titles include *Deepstep Come Shining, Just Whistle, Tremble,* and *Translations of the Gospel Back Into Tongues.* She has won numerous awards, including a Lannan Literary Award and the Witter Bynner Prize for poetry from the American Academy and Institute of Arts and Letters. She has been recipient of fellowships from the Bunting Institute, the Guggenheim Foundation, the Lila Wallace Foundation (through which she undertook the Lost Roads Project, a chronicle of the poetry and poets of Arkansas), the Whiting and the National Endowment for the Arts. She is currently State Poet of Rhode Island.

New Issues Poetry & Prose

Editor, Herbert Scott

James Armstrong, *Monument In A Summer Hat*
Michael Burkard, *Pennsylvania Collection Agency*
Anthony Butts, *Fifth Season*
Kevin Cantwell, *Something Black in the Green Part of Your Eye*
Gladys Cardiff, *A Bare Unpainted Table*
Kevin Clark, *In the Evening of No Warning*
Jim Daniels, *Night with Drive-By Shooting Stars*
Joseph Featherstone, *Brace's Cove*
Lisa Fishman, *The Deep Heart's Core Is a Suitcase*
Robert Grunst, *The Smallest Bird in North America*
Mark Halperin, *Time as Distance*
Myronn Hardy, *Approaching the Center*
Edward Haworth Hoeppner, *Rain Through High Windows*
Cynthia Hogue, *Flux*
Janet Kauffman, *Rot* (fiction)
Josie Kearns, *New Numbers*
Maurice Kilwein Guevara, *Autobiography of So-and-so: Poems in Prose*
Ruth Ellen Kocher, *When the Moon Knows You're Wandering*
Steve Langan, *Freezing*
Lance Larsen, *Erasable Walls*
David Dodd Lee, *Downsides of Fish Culture*
Deanne Lundin, *The Ginseng Hunter's Notebook*
Joy Manesiotis, *They Sing to Her Bones*
Sarah Mangold, *Household Mechanics*
David Marlatt, *A Hog Slaughtering Woman*
Paula McLain, *Less of Her*
Sarah Messer, *Bandit Letters*
Malena Mörling, *Ocean Avenue*
Julie Moulds, *The Woman with a Cubed Head*
Marsha de la O, *Black Hope*
C. Mikal Oness, *Water Becomes Bone*
Elizabeth Powell, *The Republic of Self*
Margaret Rabb, *Granite Dives*
Rebecca Reynolds, *Daughter of the Hangnail*
Martha Rhodes, *Perfect Disappearance*
Beth Roberts, *Brief Moral History in Blue*